Bradshaw's Railway Diary 2016

This diary belongs to

....

PENKRIDGE.

...I don't like the look of these tramroads;
there's mischief in them.

The Duke of Bridgewater, a prominent canal owner, *c.* 1825

Let no one, unless he has stood on the bridge
at Liverpool Street, say, at 9 o'clock in the morning
or 6 o'clock in the evening, ever suppose he knows what
suburban traffic really can be.

W. M. Acworth, *The Railways of England*, 1899

Published in Great Britain in 2015 by Old House books & maps
c/o Osprey Publishing, PO Box 883, Oxford OX2 9PH, UK.
c/o Osprey Publishing, PO Box 3985, New York,
NY 10185-3985, USA.
Website: www.oldhousebooks.co.uk

© 2015 Old House

A CIP catalogue record for this book is available from the
British Library.
ISBN-13: 978 1 78366 042 1
Compiled by David Turner.

Title page image: The London and North Western Railway's
Birmingham New Street Station in around 1900.

'Diary belongs to' image: Penkridge on the Grand Junction
Railway in 1839.

Unless otherwise credited, all pictures belong to David Turner.

Printed in China through World Print Ltd.
14 15 16 17 18   10 9 8 7 6 5 4 3 2 1

CALENDAR 2016

January

M	T	W	T	F	S	S
				1	2	3
4	5	6	7	8	9	10
11	12	13	14	15	16	17
18	19	20	21	22	23	24
25	26	27	28	29	30	31

February

M	T	W	T	F	S	S
1	2	3	4	5	6	7
8	9	10	11	12	13	14
15	16	17	18	19	20	21
22	23	24	25	26	27	28
29						

March

M	T	W	T	F	S	S
	1	2	3	4	5	6
7	8	9	10	11	12	13
14	15	16	17	18	19	20
21	22	23	24	25	26	27
28	29	30	31			

April

M	T	W	T	F	S	S
				1	2	3
4	5	6	7	8	9	10
11	12	13	14	15	16	17
18	19	20	21	22	23	24
25	26	27	28	29	30	

May

M	T	W	T	F	S	S
						1
2	3	4	5	6	7	8
9	10	11	12	13	14	15
16	17	18	19	20	21	22
23	24	25	26	27	28	29
30	31					

June

M	T	W	T	F	S	S
		1	2	3	4	5
6	7	8	9	10	11	12
13	14	15	16	17	18	19
20	21	22	23	24	25	26
27	28	29	30			

July

M	T	W	T	F	S	S
				1	2	3
4	5	6	7	8	9	10
11	12	13	14	15	16	17
18	19	20	21	22	23	24
25	26	27	28	29	30	31

August

M	T	W	T	F	S	S
1	2	3	4	5	6	7
8	9	10	11	12	13	14
15	16	17	18	19	20	21
22	23	24	25	26	27	28
29	30	31				

September

M	T	W	T	F	S	S
			1	2	3	4
5	6	7	8	9	10	11
12	13	14	15	16	17	18
19	20	21	22	23	24	25
26	27	28	29	30		

October

M	T	W	T	F	S	S
					1	2
3	4	5	6	7	8	9
10	11	12	13	14	15	16
17	18	19	20	21	22	23
24	25	26	27	28	29	30
31						

November

M	T	W	T	F	S	S
	1	2	3	4	5	6
7	8	9	10	11	12	13
14	15	16	17	18	19	20
21	22	23	24	25	26	27
28	29	30				

December

M	T	W	T	F	S	S
			1	2	3	4
5	6	7	8	9	10	11
12	13	14	15	16	17	18
19	20	21	22	23	24	25
26	27	28	29	30	31	

CALENDAR 2017

January

M	T	W	T	F	S	S
						1
2	3	4	5	6	7	8
9	10	11	12	13	14	15
16	17	18	19	20	21	22
23	24	25	26	27	28	29
30	31					

February

M	T	W	T	F	S	S
		1	2	3	4	5
6	7	8	9	10	11	12
13	14	15	16	17	18	19
20	21	22	23	24	25	26
27	28					

March

M	T	W	T	F	S	S
		1	2	3	4	5
6	7	8	9	10	11	12
13	14	15	16	17	18	19
20	21	22	23	24	25	26
27	28	29	30	31		

April

M	T	W	T	F	S	S
					1	2
3	4	5	6	7	8	9
10	11	12	13	14	15	16
17	18	19	20	21	22	23
24	25	26	27	28	29	30

May

M	T	W	T	F	S	S
1	2	3	4	5	6	7
8	9	10	11	12	13	14
15	16	17	18	19	20	21
22	23	24	25	26	27	28
29	30	31				

June

M	T	W	T	F	S	S
			1	2	3	4
5	6	7	8	9	10	11
12	13	14	15	16	17	18
19	20	21	22	23	24	25
26	27	28	29	30		

July

M	T	W	T	F	S	S
					1	2
3	4	5	6	7	8	9
10	11	12	13	14	15	16
17	18	19	20	21	22	23
24	25	26	27	28	29	30
31						

August

M	T	W	T	F	S	S
	1	2	3	4	5	6
7	8	9	10	11	12	13
14	15	16	17	18	19	20
21	22	23	24	25	26	27
28	29	30	31			

September

M	T	W	T	F	S	S
				1	2	3
4	5	6	7	8	9	10
11	12	13	14	15	16	17
18	19	20	21	22	23	24
25	26	27	28	29	30	

October

M	T	W	T	F	S	S
						1
2	3	4	5	6	7	8
9	10	11	12	13	14	15
16	17	18	19	20	21	22
23	24	25	26	27	28	29
30	31					

November

M	T	W	T	F	S	S
	1	2	3	4	5	
6	7	8	9	10	11	12
13	14	15	16	17	18	19
20	21	22	23	24	25	26
27	28	29	30			

December

M	T	W	T	F	S	S
				1	2	3
4	5	6	7	8	9	10
11	12	13	14	15	16	17
18	19	20	21	22	23	24
25	26	27	28	29	30	31

TRAVELLING FOR WORK

_———৩ • ৫———_

At the start of the railway age, in the 1830s, long commutes to work were a rarity for the majority of the population, who mostly worked close to their homes. For this reason suburbs were not a common feature of most towns. On the other hand, most major cities had developed them in some form. In London, areas such as St John's Wood, Belgravia, Brixton and Camberwell were already established as 'suburbs', while in Liverpool housing along the seashore from Southport to Hoylake served the same purpose. Manchester's suburbs were located at Pendleton, Rusholme and Newton Heath.

The creation of railway connections did not immediately develop the 'commute' and the suburb. Indeed, before 1870 much of the inner suburban growth of cities was not due to the coming of the railways. Areas in Glasgow such as Langside, Pollockshields and Kelvinside, only 2 or 3 miles from the centre, developed without railway communication, while in Liverpool the bulk of suburban growth in the mid-century took place independent of railway development. Birmingham's inner suburbs of New Hall, Edgbaston and Islington were also not a product of the railways.

In many places travel into work from an outer region of a city was undertaken by other means. From the 1830s until the 1870s the Birmingham Omnibus Conveyance Company and the Midland Omnibus Company stimulated the growth of suburban areas because they dominated transport across the city. The railway's limited role in the development of inner suburbs was highlighted by a government report of 1854. Of those travelling into London daily, around 200,000 went by foot, approximately 26,000 used the omnibuses, fifteen thousand used the steamboat from places such as Greenwich and London (both of which had a railway connection) and only between six and ten thousand used two main-line stations.

A Great Eastern Railway poster promoting the 'healthy district' of Harlow Garden Village to commuters. (Science and Society Picture Library)

The reason the railways had only limited impact on the development of commuting and suburbs before 1870 varied from place to place and cannot be attributed to any particular factor. Many early railways did not consider the development of commuter traffic a worthwhile or profitable endeavour. When the London & Birmingham line opened in 1838, the first station was at Harrow, 11 miles away from Euston; the directors were considering only the needs of the long-distance traveller. Also, cheap fares or early trains that might have attracted commuters were not provided in the early days. Even for many

Commuters board a train at Coombe & Malden, in south-west London, in around 1910. (Tony Harden)

comfortably-off middle-class people, the cost of travelling into the city for work by train was prohibitive.

There were areas, however, where railways were a powerful stimulant of suburban development before 1870. The London to Greenwich Railway was largely promoted as a commuter railway. In 1833 an 'Inhabitant of Greenwich' wrote that 'when the railway is open, this neighbourhood will be greatly enlarged ... that the speed with which the inhabitants can be conveyed from the smoke of the city to the pure air of Blackheath and Shooter's Hill will be a great inducement to the occupation of houses on this side of London.' Other similar lines followed, such as the Newcastle & North Shields Railway. Most of these lines were well patronised: in 1842–3 the London & Greenwich was carrying around twelve thousand people, mainly from the middle classes, every weekday. However, their financial performance was poor.

Other railways, especially those serving London, soon built branch lines off their main lines specifically to serve middle-class commuters. The London & South Western Railway, whose original main line ran between London and Southampton, constructed branches to Richmond (later extended to Windsor) and Hampton Court, which opened in 1844 and 1849 respectively. In other places suburbs grew up around mainlines because of the actions of enthusiastic property developers. The most famous of these places was Kingston-on-Railway, which was on the L&SWR main line and is now known as 'Surbiton'.

From the 1860s reductions in fares also helped to expand the suburbs, allowing better-paid working people to leave behind the densely packed housing of the city and to move further out from the centre. The underground lines, which were expensive to build and needed to run with full trains to be profitable, in 1864 started running two trains daily from Hammersmith to the City on weekday mornings at 5.30 and 5.40, charging a fare of only 3d return. So successful were they that at the close of 1865 1,800 and two thousand workmen respectively were using them daily.

Parliament also played a role in developing commuting. When constructing their lines through cities, the railways demolished the houses of working people, forcing many of them to move into overcrowded accommodation elsewhere. Public outcry at these hardships led Parliament to act. It started by compelling the railways through their authorising Acts of Parliament to provide cheap trains for working people, so that they could relocate further from their place of work. The first company receiving one of these orders was the Great Eastern Railway in 1864 when it extended its line to Liverpool Street. The Act stated that it was to provide workmen's trains to London from Edmonton and Walthamstow at a return cost of 2d. Then in 1883 came the Cheap Trains Act. Designed to encourage the 'migration of the working classes into the suburbs', it removed the passenger duty on any train charging less than a penny a mile and gave the Board of Trade powers to order the railway companies to operate a larger number of cheap trains. By 1899 104 workmen's trains ran daily, usually very early in the morning, returning late at night.

Despite what we know, the extent to which the railways influenced the development of the suburb and the commute before 1914 is unclear. The railways undoubtedly broke down some obstacles to suburban migration after 1870: the population of central London fell into sharp decline in the 1880s. But suburban growth in most places was not necessarily the result of a railway. Edgar Harper, the London County Council's statistical officer, was asked in 1906 how he accounted for the growth of London's outer southern suburbs, given that train services were not good and the fares were high. He responded that 'a part of the growth must fairly be ascribed to the growth of old towns independent of the provision of railway facilities to central London'. This reflected that not everyone who lived in the suburbs commuted into the city for work, and railway suburbs were rarely established in open fields arbitrarily. They tended to cluster round existing settlements, where a nucleus of skills and services already existed and then grew.

David Turner

While heavy snowfalls could potentially be very disruptive for train services, railway managers' major concern was that they increased the risk of accident. In winter months it was not uncommon for trains to get stuck in heavy snow drifts, as shown in this case from 1850, creating an obstacle on the line. Drivers' visibility was also limited in snowstorms, increasing the likelihood that they would miss signals or not see a stuck train ahead. To mitigate the danger of a train running into the rear of a standing one, the guard of any stationary train was instructed to run back and place small explosive detonators on the rail. When a following train rolled over them the detonator would explode, alerting its driver to the danger ahead and causing him to put on the brake. Theoretically at least, this prevented a smash occurring. (Picture: Science and Society Picture Library)

Monday

28

Tuesday

29

Wednesday

30

Thursday

31

New Year's Day

Friday

1

Saturday

2

Sunday

3

DO NOT SNIGGER

Among the passengers who recently got into the London train at Three Bridges were a bride and bridegroom of the regular 'hollyhock' order. It was one of the old-fashioned third-class carriages, open from end to end, and although it was full of passengers, the pair began to squeeze hands and hug as soon as they were seated. This, of course, attracted attention, and pretty soon everybody was nodding and winking, and several persons so far forgot themselves as to laugh outright. By-and-bye the broad-shouldered and red-haired groom became aware of the fact that he was being ridiculed, and stretched himself to the height of six feet, looked up and down and said: 'There seems to be considerable nodding and winking around here because I'm hugging the girl who was married to me this morning. If the rules of this railway forbid a man from hugging his wife after he's paid full fare, then I'm going to get out at the next station; but if the rules don't, and this winking and blinking isn't bitten right off when we pass the next telegraph post, I'm going to begin on the front seats and create a rising market for false teeth and crutches.' If there were any more winks and blinks in that carriage the groom did not see them.

Great Western Railway Magazine, October 1897

Bank holiday (Scotland)

Monday

4

Tuesday

5

Wednesday

6

Thursday

7

Friday

8

Saturday

9

Sunday

10

A Train in 1837 for Second Class Outside Passengers.

LONDON & NORTH W. RAILWAY COMP

Over the Victorian period the passenger experience changed immensely. Were you to board a train in 1837, as the top images depict, the accommodation would have been cramped, second- and third-class passengers would likely have had hard, wooden seats, suspension was basic, and there would have been no heating. Third-class passengers would also have to deal with the elements; most carriages provided for them were 'open' at the sides and a roof was a rarity. By the 1890s and early twentieth century the situation had changed greatly for all classes of passenger. All carriages were enclosed, suspension was commonplace, most had heating and lighting, and the uncomfortable inconvenience of hard seats was a thing of memory. Accordingly, in 1907 Arnold Bennett wrote in *The Grim Smile of the Five Towns* that 'Happily the third class carriages on the London & North Western Railway are pretty comfortable'.

Monday

11

Tuesday

12

Wednesday

13

Thursday

14

Friday

15

Saturday

16

Sunday

17

Monday
18

Tuesday
19

Wednesday
20

Thursday
21

Friday
22

Saturday
23

Sunday
24

This map shows the lines of the Metropolitan Railway and the Metropolitan and District Railway in 1882.
(British Library Creative Commons)

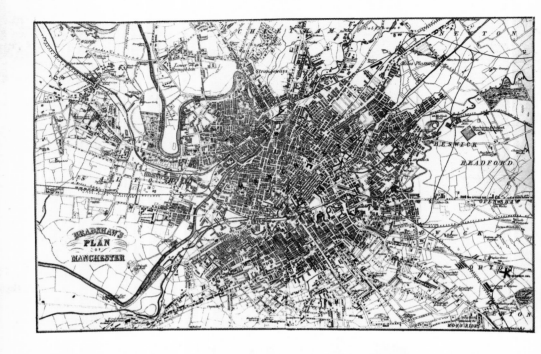

MANCHESTER

MANCHESTER, the metropolis of the cotton manufacture [sic], a cathedral city, and parliamentary borough, in the south-east corner of Lancashire, on the Irwell, 188¼ miles from London, and 31½ from Liverpool. The last named town is the real port which supplies its staple article in the raw state, but Manchester itself has all the privileges of one, being licensed to bond imported goods as much as if it were by the sea side. It has been the head of a bishop's see since 1848, when a new diocese was taken out of Chester, including the greater part of Lancashire; and the Collegiate Church turned into a cathedral.

Among the factories, notice Birley's, at Chorlton, and Dewhurst's, in the Adelphi, Salford, with its tall stone chimney, 243 feet high, on a base 21 feet square and 45 feet high. The bleach and dye works are placed up and down the Irwell and its tributaries. Wood and Westhead's smallware manufactory, Brook Street; Whitworth's machine factory in Chorlton Street; Sharp's, Atlas Works, Oxford Street; Fairbairn's, in Ancoats; Nasmyth's, Bridgewater Foundry, at Patricroft, may be visited. Manchester is famed for its magnificent warehouses. For style of architecture and beauty, perhaps Watts's new warehouses in Portland Street excel all others, and ought by all means to be seen.

Bradshaw's Handbook, 1863.

Burns' Night

Monday

25

Tuesday

26

Wednesday

27

Thursday

28

Friday

29

Saturday

30

Sunday

31

"'WE'RE AWFULLY LATE,' HE WAS SAYING."

FEBRUARY

Monday

1

Tuesday

2

Wednesday

3

Thursday

4

Friday

5

Saturday

6

Sunday

7

This image, taken from an 1893 novel, depicts passengers alighting from a first-class carriage.
(British Library Creative Commons)

MONKEY HUNT — AMUSING SCENE IN THE CITY

·

An amusing scene was witnessed at Liverpool Street Station on Friday morning, as the result of two monkeys escaping from custody. They arrived in a crate from the Continent, and while waiting outside the parcels office in Bishopsgate-street to be conveyed to their owner in the East End, they re-gained their liberty by destroying part of the crate.

They climbed to the iron girders of the station roof, and although a large number of railway employees engaged in the hunt, it was fully two hours before the animals were re-captured. Many attempts to secure them failed, the monkeys, in a tantalising fashion, jumping on to other girders when their pursuers were about to pounce upon them.

One of the animals jumped through a window of Hamilton House, but its stay was brief, the hubbub of station life being apparently more to its liking.

Western Gazette, Friday 14 October 1910

Liverpool Street Station, 1907.

Monday
8

Tuesday
9

Wednesday
10

Thursday
11

Friday
12

Saturday
13

Valentine's Day

Sunday
14

Monday

15

Tuesday

16

Wednesday

17

Thursday

18

Friday

19

Saturday

20

Sunday

21

An advertisement for the Metropolitan District Railway from 1888, which highlights the many and varied attractions along its line. (British Library Creative Commons)

A COLD EUSTON STATION

No sound is heard in the cold air but the hissing of a pilot engine, which, like a restless spirit advancing and retrograding, is stealing along the intermediate rails, waiting to carry off the next down-train; its course being marked by white steam meandering above it and by red-hot coals of different sizes which are continually falling from beneath it. In this obscure scene the Company's interminable lines of gaslights (there are 232 at the Euston Station), economically screwed down to the minimum of existence, are feebly illuminating the damp varnished panels of the line of carriages in waiting, the brass door handles of the cabs, the shining haims, brass browbands and other ornaments on the drooping heads and motionless backs of the cab-horses; and while the blood-red signal lamp is glaring near the tunnel to deter unauthorised intrusion, the stars of heaven cast a faint silvery light through the long strips of plate-glass in the roof above the platform. On a sudden is heard – the stranger hardly knows whence – the mysterious moan of compressed air, followed by the violent ringing of a bell. That instant every gaslight on and above a curve of 900 feet suddenly bursts into full power. The carriages, cabs, &c. appear, comparatively speaking, in broad daylight, and the beautiful iron reticulation which sustains the glazed roof appears like fairy work.

Sir Francis Head, *Stokers and Pokers*, 1849

Monday

22

Tuesday

23

Wednesday

24

Thursday

25

Friday

26

Saturday

27

Sunday

28

Monday

29

St David's Day

Tuesday

1

Wednesday

2

Thursday

3

Friday

4

Saturday

5

Mothering Sunday

Sunday

6

Detail of a painting of the Liverpool station of the Liverpool & Manchester Railway, 1833.
(Stapleton Collection / The Bridgeman Art Library)

The station at York is one of the most important on the British railway network because of its key position as a railway junction approximately halfway between London and Edinburgh. A temporary wooden building was all the city received when the railways came to York in 1839, but this was soon superseded by a permanent station building inside the city walls in 1841. However, as the railway network grew, and an increasing number of trains travelled from London to the North via the East Coast Main Line, the need for them to reverse out of the station at York to continue their onward journey had by the late 1860s become irksome. The current station, designed by the North Eastern Railway's architects Thomas Prosser and William Peachey, was opened in 1877. At the time it was the largest passenger station in the world.

Monday

7

Tuesday

8

Wednesday

9

Thursday

10

Friday

11

Saturday

12

Sunday

13

RAILWAY WAIFS AND STRAYS

GENTLEMEN who *will* look out of the windows of railway carriages to see 'what's the matter,' and get their hats knocked off and left behind at the rate of fifty miles an hour; third-class young Ladies who *will* hold parasols over their complexions on windy days, and let them go ballooning down the line at hurricane time; Dandies who won't look after their own luggage, but leave everything to 'those fellows, the porters,' and so lose it; Wives who *will* terminate their journeys at the terminus in their husband's arms, regardless of their 'trifles from Tunbridge' packed up in pretty baskets; Commercial travellers who forget their samples; Gents who rush away without their canes; Aunts who leave behind their umbrellas; Nieces oblivious of their pattens; in short, everybody who misses, or forgets, or leaves behind, or loses anything on a railway, may consider it nearly as safe as if they had not been stupid or careless, or in too great a hurry, or forgetful; – and have a much better chance of finding it than if they had never stirred away from home. To the terminus of most railways is attached what the French would call an *administration* or *service* – a warehouse and a staff of clerks and porters – for the deposit and restoration of the lost or left behind; which, for the variety and value, would put to shame the dazzling and heterogeneous treasures of Don Rolando's Cave.

Charles Dickens (editor), *Household Words: conducted by Charles Dickens*, 28 December 1850

Monday

14

Tuesday

15

Wednesday

16

Thursday

17

Friday

18

Saturday

19

Sunday

20

TERRIFIC EXPLOSION IN THE GREAT NORTHERN RAILWAY STATION

•

On Tuesday morning a fearful explosion took place in the Newark station yard of the Great Northern Railway, just as the 7.44 am train was about starting north. The passengers had taken their seats, and the whistle had sounded, when, in a moment, a most alarming explosion took place, with a report that might be heard for miles distant. The brass dome on the top of the boiler, with which the safety valve is connected, was blown direct in the air, a height of 30 or 40 yards, and the main part of it fell through the roof of the platform on the same side of the station yard, thirty yards or so from the place where the engine was standing... Providently, no one was injured.

Nottinghamshire Guardian – Thursday, 25 October 1860

Newark station, 1910.

Monday

21

Tuesday

22

Wednesday

23

Thursday

24

Good Friday

Friday

25

Saturday

26

Easter Sunday

Sunday

27

'A TYPICAL HOTSPUR CROWD'

THROUGHOUT the winter season many thousands of enthusiasts are conveyed by the Great Eastern Railway to witness those exciting struggles for supremacy which take place week by week between the various great professional football organizations. Yet few ... give one moment's serious consideration to the hard work and careful forethought necessary on the part of the railway officials to perfect and carry out the intricate arrangements for conveying these huge crowds of shouting, cheering partisans to the various scenes of action.

Some weeks prior to the date of one of these big 'home' matches ... a railway representative confers with the club's officials, and the magnitude of the crowd which may be expected is roughly gauged by reference to the records of former games. The number of passengers which will travel by the various routes has then to be computed, and the all-important question, 'How many "Specials" will suffice?' is thereupon settled.

In addition to the White Hart Lane arrangements, cheap tickets are issued to Park Station on match days, from Hertford, Ware, St Margarets, Rye House, and all points between Ponders End and Broxbourne, the results proving that these concessions are amply justified.

The work progresses step by step, until the day of the 'big engagement' arrives.

Standing upon the west side of the bridge which spans our great terminus, on a 'Cup-tie' Saturday when Tottenham ... is 'at home' to some equally famous rival from the North or Midlands, one can watch the constant stream of 'football devotees' trickling through the barriers as the first 'White Hart Lane Special' draws in. This 'stream' rapidly swells into a torrent – a flood – as the hands of the big clock advance and the factories, warehouses, and offices of our mighty city open their portals and release hordes of busy workers.

Trainload follows trainload... A snatch of song, or perhaps a comic chorus, intermingle with the loud jests and banter of the noisy contingent; whilst the quieter element settles down with difficulty to 'talk' football. The chances of the rival teams are carefully weighed, the individual players criticized or praised, and the prices of the latest additions to the 'transfer list' are debated as eagerly as stockbrokers might discuss the variations in 'home rails'.

Great Eastern Railway Magazine, March 1912

Easter Monday (UK, exc Scotland)

Monday
28

Tuesday
29

Wednesday
30

Thursday
31

Friday
1

Saturday
2

Sunday
3

TRAVELLING FOR CULTURE

The popularity of cultural entertainments, for example the theatre, music festivals, museums and exhibitions, developed significantly over the nineteenth and early twentieth centuries, and the railways were in many instances an important factor in this change.

Urban theatres benefited significantly from railway connections in the nineteenth century, as hundreds of thousands of customers were transported yearly to them from suburban and out-of town districts. It is unclear how many people used the railway for this purpose, although the number of visitors to theatres from the provinces increased rapidly. Theatre managers as a result had to accommodate their needs. E .T. Smith, manager of the Drury Lane Theatre, stated in 1866 that he tried to conclude his programme at a 'reasonable hour' so that patrons could catch the 11 o'clock train home. Similarly, J. B. Buckstone of the Haymarket proclaimed that 'I can also tell when a quantity of people have come from the surrounding districts; at a certain time you can see them moving away to catch the trains home'. These theatregoers, who had clearly shunned cheaper local

CHEAP FARES on EARLY CLOSING DAYS.
For full Particulars, see PAMPHLETS

LOW FARES for SCHOOL, CLUBS AND WORKS EXCURSIONS

LUGGAGE COLLECTED, CONVEYED AND DELIVERED 1/- PER PACKAGE.

LUGGAGE IN ADVANCE.

LUGGAGE CONVEYED AND DELIVERED 6d. PER PACKAGE.

CARTED LUGGAGE

PARCELS CONVEYED TO ALL PARTS

CHEAP RATES
FREE COLLECTION.
Quick Transit and Delivery

REDUCED RATES FOR FARM and DAIRY PRODUCE by Passenger Train.

Great Western Railway.

EXCURSIONS TO THE . . PANTOMIMES, &c.

Bristol Amusements, etc.

PRINCES THEATRE, Park Row—Pantomime "JACK HORNER."
THEATRE ROYAL, King Street—Pantomime "DICK WHITTINGTON."
PALACE THEATRE, Baldwin Street—VARIETY ENTERTAINMENT—Two Performances Nightly.
EMPIRE THEATRE, Old Market Street—VARIETY ENTERTAINMENT—Two Performances Nightly.
COLSTON HALL, Park's Menagerie and Variety Entertainment.
ELECTRIC THEATRES and SKATING RINKS.
BRISTOL MUSEUM, Queen's Road—Admission Free. | During hours open.

On Thursday, January 26th, 1911
An EXCURSION TRAIN will run to

BRISTOL
(TEMPLE MEADS STATION).

FROM	Times of Starting	Return Fares, 3rd Class	Returning the same evening from Temple Meads Station at
	p.m.	s. d.	
Wellington ...	1 15	8 9	
Taunton ...	1 45	2 6	
Durston ...	1 55	2 6	
Bridgwater ...	2 5	2 6	
Dunball ...	2 15	2 6	p.m.
Highbridge ...	2 25	2 3	
Brent Knoll ...	2 30	2 0	11-35
Bleadon and Uphill ...	2 40	2 0	
Weston-S-Mare (General Station) ...	2 50	1 6	
Clevedon A ...	3 27	1 3	
Yatton ...	3 55	1 3	
BRISTOL (Temple Meads) arr.	3 30	—	

A—These passengers arrive Bristol (Temple Meads) at 4·25 p.m.

NO LUGGAGE ALLOWED.

Children under 3 years of age, free ; 3 and under 12, half-price.

The Tickets are not transferable. Should an Excursion Ticket be used for any other Station than those named upon it, or by any other Train than as herein specified, it will be rendered void, and therefore the fare paid will be liable to forfeiture and the full ordinary fare will become chargeable.

Bristol Station Refreshment Rooms will be open for Refreshments to bona-fide Passengers on Return journey.

For any further information respecting the arrangements shewn in this bill, application should be made at any of the Company's Offices or Agencies ; to M.W. BOWED, Divisional Superintendent, G.W.R., St. David's Station, Exeter ; to Mr C.KISLINGBURY, Divisional Superintendent, Temple Meads Station, Bristol ; or to Mr G. ALDINGBURY, Superintendent of the Line, G.W.R., Paddington Station,W.

Paddington, Dec., 1910.   JAMES C. INGLIS, General Manager.
857—Royal 8vo.— E—4000—D.R. 55.   B—8000—20.

206   Latimer, Trend & Co., Printers, 165, Union Street, Plymouth

entertainments, were undoubtedly middle-class. Nonetheless, by the early 1900s many others from working-class backgrounds would walk or take the tube or omnibus to wait patiently outside central London theatres, sometimes in rain, sleet or snow, for the 'unbookable pit or gallery seats'.

On the other hand, not all central London theatres benefited from the new rail links to suburban districts. Waterloo station, which served the suburbs of south-west London, had northern-facing exits, resulting in passengers being brought closer to theatre land: the Lyceum, Drury Lane and the eastern end of the Strand. The result was that patronage of the Victoria Theatre (now the Old Vic), which was to the south of the station, mostly came from local sources. The developing popularity of suburban theatres and music-halls from the 1880s was also not a product of the railways. Most of their trade was local, and audiences preferred to journey to them by foot, cart, omnibus and, later on, by tram.

Other cultural activities, for example museums and music festivals, also benefited from railways, enabling out-of-town and suburban dwellers to travel into large cities to visit them. But it was the reduced-fare excursion train, which started to appear in the 1830s, that became particularly popular amongst those from all classes engaging in cultural pursuits, conveying them to music concerts, grand exhibitions, or cities for days out (in addition to visits to the seaside). The *Sheffield & Rotherham Independent* reported in April 1841 that during that year's Whitsuntide holidays the North Midland Railway would operate 'an excursion train from Sheffield to Derby, when no doubt thousands of our townsmen will take the opportunity of visiting that pleasant town and its arboretum'. As a testament to the popularity of such excursions, by 1865 three railways, the Lancashire & Yorkshire, the London & North Western and the Midland Railway, carried 1.1 million excursion passengers between them. To a large extent this popularity developed because the cheap excursion fares the railways offered allowed many working-class people to take part in tourism and leisure activities for the first time.

The high point of the early excursion train was its role in bringing people to the 'Great Exhibition of the Works of Industry of All Nations', which was held in the Crystal Palace between 1 May and 15 October 1851. Travel agents, including the noted excursion organiser Thomas Cook, and independent groups arranged excursions to the exhibition from as far afield as Yorkshire. Some organisations even set up 'exhibition clubs' to arrange the trips. Such was the exhibition's appeal that all the companies serving London experienced considerable increases in passenger numbers; the Great Western's passenger traffic increased by 38.3 per cent that year and Thomas Cook claimed that, acting as an agent, he had brought 165,000 individuals into Euston.

After the 1871 Bank Holiday Act, which established four national holidays, the number of excursions the railways operated continued to expand and long-distance excursions were put on more regularly. For example, in June 1877 the Midland Railway ran an excursion train from Bradford via Shipley, Leeds, Normanton, Barnsley, Cudworth, Swinton and Masborough to the one-day Handel Festival at Crystal Palace. First- and third-class passengers could buy their tickets with or without admission to the festival included in the price. Whether the railway companies benefited from the additional income received from excursions is unknown, although between 1901 and 1909 over ten per cent of the London, Brighton & South Coast

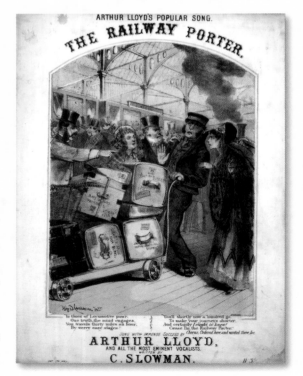

Front cover of sheet music for C. Slowman's popular Victorian music-hall song entitled 'The Railway Porter', made famous by the singer Arthur Lloyd. (Science and Society Picture Library)

Railway's passenger revenue was generated by excursions.

It was not only the audiences who valued railway connections: the performers did too. Touring artistes were a common feature in the late eighteenth and early nineteenth centuries, with strolling players looking for venues wherever they might find them. But the touring companies of the railway era were very different. There were two kinds. The first kind would tour with a successful West End hit and then disband. The earliest of these operated around the 1860s, with the railway system allowing provincial touring to become an integral part of the British theatre scene. The second type of touring company travelled around with a repertory of acts. These were unstable enterprises, and usually remained in existence only as long as the money and management were available. Yet in no small part because of the railway network, their number grew in the late-Victorian period: in 1871 around twelve were touring, by 1896 *The Era* listed 158.

Many railways saw the virtue of supporting these companies and ran special trains for them. On 3 February 1895 the London & South Western Railway conveyed Morgan's Pantomime Company from Portsmouth to Cardiff via Basingstoke. Departing at 9.35 a.m., their train conveyed the whole company, with two third-class carriages carrying the artistes, while the one horse box and four open trucks doubtless carried scenery and props.

The railways therefore had a notable impact on the cultural life of Britain. They brought thousands of individuals to central theatres, festivals, exhibitions and museums, gave rise to the excursion trains that allowed many working-class people to attend cultural entertainments previously unavailable to them, and facilitated the movement of touring theatre companies.

David Turner

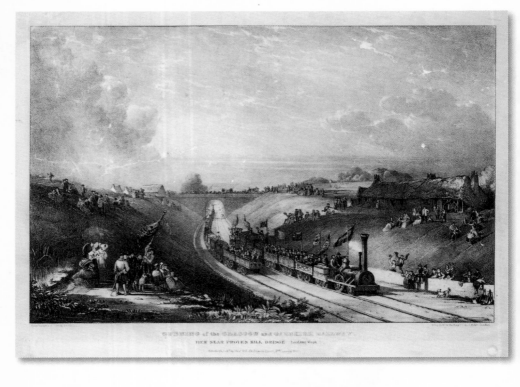

OPENING of the GLASGOW and GREENOCK RAILWAY.
VIEW NEAR PROVEN MILL BRIDGE. Looking West.

GLASGOW

That which was the ruin of many small places in this part of Great Britain, namely the Union, 1707, was the grand cause of the prosperity of Glasgow, which from its admirable position on a fine navigable river in the heart of a coal-field, and from the spirit of the inhabitants, has risen to be reckoned as the fourth port of the United Kingdom, and a rival to Manchester. When Bailie Nicol Jarvie and his worthy father, the deacon, 'praise to his memory', lived in the Salt Market, before the American revolution, it was a great place for the tobacco trade, but since 1792 cotton has been the staple business.

Population about 329,097, of which perhaps 50,000 are employed in the spinning, weaving, bleaching, and dyeing of cotton goods, worsted, muslin, silks, &c., while a large number are engaged in the manufacture of iron, brass, steam engines, glass, nails, pottery, umbrellas, hats, chemicals, and other branches of trade, and in wooden and iron ship building, besides numbers engaged in maritime and commercial transactions. These are the distinguishing characteristics of modern Glasgow, and the commercial activity and restlessness of its inhabitants have caused the immense impulse its trade has received within the last fifty years.

Bradshaw's Handbook, 1863.

Monday

4

Tuesday

5

Wednesday

6

Thursday

7

Friday

8

Saturday

9

Sunday

10

Abraham Solomon's painting *Second Class – The Parting*, from 1855, shows a young boy being comforted in a railway carriage by his mother while a relative looks on. The posters in the background suggest he is either emigrating to Australia or about to join the Merchant Navy. (Picture: Science and Society Picture Library)

Monday

11

Tuesday

12

Wednesday

13

Thursday

14

Friday

15

Saturday

16

Sunday

17

THE SLOW TRAIN

On Southern lines the trains which crawl
Deliberately to and fro
Make life a burden; of them all
This is the slowest of the slow.
Impatiently condemned to bear
What is indeed an awful bore,
I've seemed to be imprisoned there
Three days, or more.

The angry passengers complain;
Of new electric cabs they talk.
They sit and swear at such a train,-
And ask, 'Shall we get out and walk?'
It's true the time seems extra long
When spent in such a wretched way,
My calculation may be wrong -
Three hours, say.

The other day I had to come
By this slow train, but facing me
Was no old buffer, dull and dumb;
I chatted with my vis-à-vis.
A pretty smile, a pretty dress,
Gay spirits no fatigue could crush;
With her it was a quick express,
Three minutes' rush.

For once I sadly left the train,
For once the time too quickly passed.
I still could angrily complain,
Why travel so absurdly fast?
At lightning speed that special went
(I'd paid the ordinary fare),
Now looking back it seems we spent
Three seconds there.

From *Mr Punch's Railway Book*, 1910

Monday
18

Tuesday
19

Wednesday
20

Thursday
21

Friday
22

St George's Day

Saturday
23

Sunday
24

INCORPORATED 16TH JULY 1846

LONDON & NORTHWESTERN Railway.

EUSTON HOTEL, LONDON.

EUSTON

EUSTON STATION, LONDON.

HOTEL TARIFF

Monday

25

Tuesday

26

Wednesday

27

Thursday

28

Friday

29

Saturday

30

Sunday

1

This elaborate hotel tariff guide was produced by the London & North Western Railway in the mid-1880s.

TRAVELLING COMPANIONS

Once I found myself racing north alone with an elderly spinster of forbidding aspect. She had long since left the 'springs of fifty years' behind. She was gaunt, grey, and bony. She wore gleaming spectacles. She was like the elderly Englishwoman dear to Parisian caricature. And the first words she uttered of sepulchral tones were these: 'I always travel in a ladies' compartment when going even the shortest journey, for you never know what might happen!' This prudent spinster, it will be seen, was gifted with that priceless possession, a vivid imagination. With her, I remember, I was moved to formulate my views as to the Ideal Train. I argued that the whole classification of passengers required immediate rearrangement. There should not only be separate carriages for children, but compartments for the newly-wed, for men who smoke inferior cigars, for schoolboys, for people who want to discuss their private affairs, for folks recovering from dangerous illnesses, for ugly people, for 'engaged' couples – or those who ought to be – for young ladies who giggle (there is no form of nerve-torture to compare to this on a long journey), and for people who regard railway travelling as an excuse for gnawing chicken-bones, drinking potent-smelling liquors, and strewing themselves and everybody else with crumbs.

Miss Hepworth Dixon, *Ladies Pictorial*, August 1896

Early May bank holiday (UK, exc Scotland)   Monday

2

Tuesday

3

Wednesday

4

Thursday

5

Friday

6

Saturday

7

Sunday

8

CREWE STATION (L & N.W. RAILWAY)

CREWE

CREWE is a railway town and first class depot, standing on the North Western main line, where the Chester, Manchester, and Staffordshire lines fall in. Formerly it was called Oak Farm, which an attorney bought for £35 an acre. The station, and many of the workmen's houses, are imitations of the Elizabethan style. Nearly 2,000 men are employed in the Company's workshops. Here are immense rolling mills for the rails, locomotive factories for the engines, including fitting-up and erecting shops, 300 feet and upwards long. An engine, with its tender, averaging £2,000, is made up of 5,416 separate pieces, and a new one is turned out every Monday morning. Wolverton is the chief hospital for repairs. At the Crewe Grease House, the yellow mixture of tallow, palm oil, and soda, used to grease the wheels is made.

Lord Crewe's seat, near at hand, is the only real remnant of antiquity, being of the age of the renaissance, introduced by Inigo Jones. It is built of brick, and is really a fine specimen of the style of architecture in the reign of James I. At the time of the civil war, it was occupied by both parties. There are some very old portraits.

Bradshaw's Handbook, 1863.

Monday

9

Tuesday

10

Wednesday

11

Thursday

12

Friday

13

Saturday

14

Sunday

15

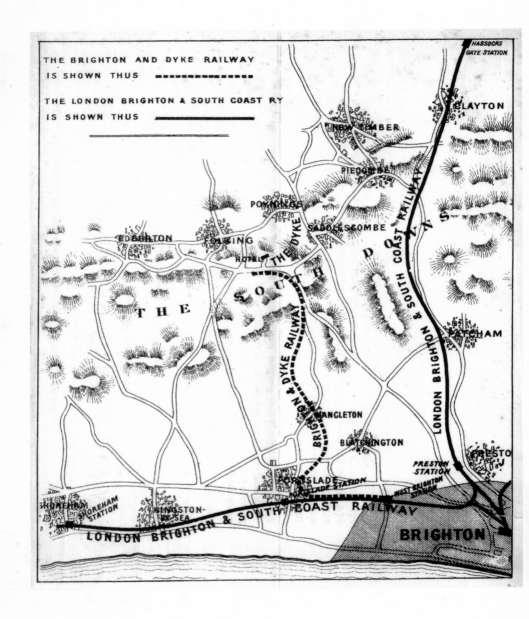

The Brighton & Dyke Railway Company was opened in 1887 to serve the very popular tourist attraction of Devil's Dyke, which at that time had two bandstands, an observatory, a camera obscura and fairground rides. On August Bank Holiday 1893 the line carried over thirty thousand people. This map is from a prospectus for the construction of the railway line from 1883. (Picture: Ian Dinmore)

Monday
16

Tuesday
17

Wednesday
18

Thursday
19

Friday
20

Saturday
21

Sunday
22

Monday

23

Tuesday

24

Wednesday

25

Thursday

26

Friday

27

Saturday

28

Sunday

29

The Great Western Railway's broad gauge locomotive Iron Duke stands at Chippenham station, Wiltshire, c. 1850, in this painting by Sean Bolan. (Science and Society Picture Library)

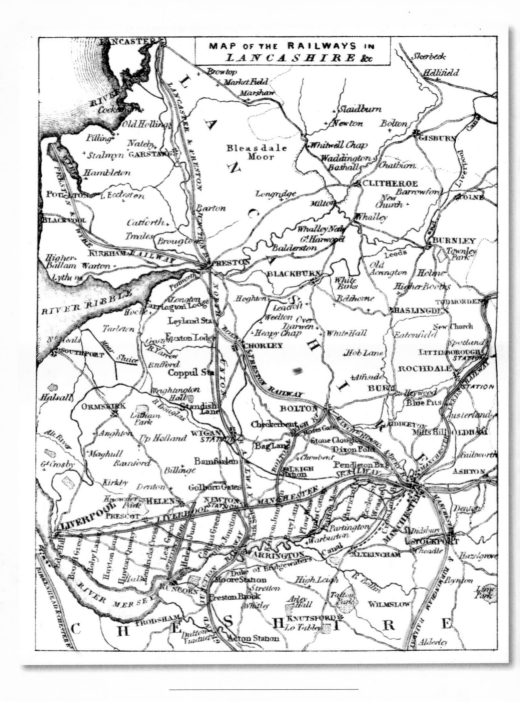

This map of the railways around Lancashire was included in only the third set of timetables issued by Bradshaw, *Bradshaw's Railway Companion*, in 1839.

Spring bank holiday (UK)   Monday

30

Tuesday

31

Wednesday

1

Thursday

2

Friday

3

Saturday

4

Sunday

5

TRAVELLING FOR HOLIDAY

—◠ • ◡—

Contrary to popular belief, the arrival of the railways did not give birth to the idea of taking a seaside holiday. By the 1830s the number of wealthy people taking long holidays had been on the rise for decades, as were the number of places they were visiting. In 1815 23,000 tourists visited Margate by sailing vessel, while fifteen years later the number arriving by steamer was 95,000. The multiplication of holiday resorts was encapsulated in Jane Austen's unfinished book *Sanditon*: 'Every five years,' proclaimed Mr Haywood, 'one hears of some new place or other starting up by the sea, and growing the fashion.'

As the popularity of seaside resorts grew, however, the railways met a growing need for transport to and from them. Interestingly, companies were not usually trying to tap potential tourist traffic when building lines to the sea; rather, it was a by-product of their creation. The line to the Fylde coast was originally built to serve the port of Fleetwood, with the lines to Blackpool and St Anne's intended only as mere branches; their importance became apparent only later. The North Wales coast became accessible only because a line was built to take passengers to the port of Holyhead. Even in the case of Brighton, the promoters of the line emphasised the all-year-round residential traffic, rather than the seasonal tourist trade.

It was also rare for the railways to create entirely new resorts. Rather, they allowed established resorts, such as Brighton, to continue to grow and prosper, while small bathing villages, such as Blackpool and Southport, became genuine resort towns for swathes of holidaymakers. Brighton is a good example of this. In the 1830s it was already a major British resort frequented by lords, ladies and occasionally royalty. The thirty-six stagecoaches daily between London and Brighton carried 117,000 people in 1835. Yet Brighton was irreversibly changed when the railways arrived in 1841. Travel by railway was much cheaper than by stagecoach and, while a coach held around fourteen people, trains could hold ten times as many. Soon the railways were conveying far more people, particularly the upper middle classes, to the resort. In the words of one commentator, Brighton was assailed by 'those swarms ... daily and weekly disgorged upon its Steyne from the cancer-like arms of the railroad'. There was even a claim that one extraordinary train from London possessed forty-four carriages, was drawn by four locomotives and carried four thousand passengers. The result was that by the mid-1840s the mass of tourists descending on Brighton each year had erased its aristocratic character forever.

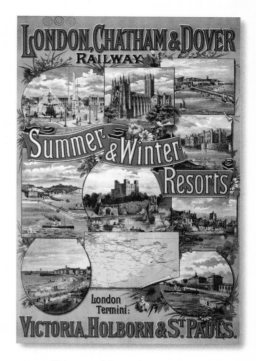

(Science and Society Picture Library)

Despite Brighton's example, the building of railways to existing resorts did not necessarily result in vast numbers of holidaymakers immediately descending on them. Scarborough

Cleethorpes, Grimsby

Cleethorpes railway station. (Tony Harden)

had been a watering-place for the wealthy long before the railways arrived. When a line was promoted to it in 1840, one objecting pamphlet expressed 'no wish for a greater influx of vagrants, and those having money to spend'. This did not happen, initially at least. When the York & Scarborough Railway was opened in 1845 the fashionability of the resort for the well-off continued and it did not lose its character for a long time after – its population remained at around 13,000 until the 1870s.

It was in the late nineteenth century that the popularity of resorts grew significantly, especially amongst the lower middle and working classes, with the numbers travelling to resorts multiplying. Massive resorts catering for these holidaymakers emerged, and places such as Blackpool, Brighton, Holyhead and Scarborough dominated the holiday market in this period. Tynemouth developed as a resort for the 'less wealthy' living in Newcastle, while Bridlington and Cleethorpes served as excursion destinations for the populations of the West Riding and Hull. One paper remarked in 1894 that 'Blackpool is to the hard-working folk of the large towns of Lancashire, what Brighton is to the moneyed classes of the Metropolis'.

The railways were the primary way that thousands of vacationers journeyed to these resorts. On the Saturday of August Bank Holiday 1899, sixty-seven special excursion trains

Passengers looking at railway advertising, 1913.

arrived in Brighton and on the Monday seventy-six arrived. Over the same weekend, 75,000 people arrived in Ramsgate by train. Some of these people may have stayed for longer than a day; others would have returned in the evening.

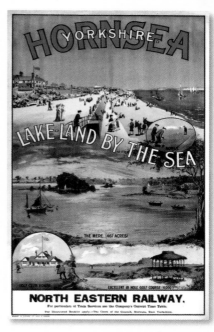

However, the railway's contribution to the development of the holiday at the seaside resort in the nineteenth century should not be overstated. The popularity of holiday resorts was already on the rise before the arrival of the railways. Growing patronage of particular resorts by the middle and working classes, particularly after 1870, was the result of a range of factors, not only the railways, including working people's rising incomes, regularity of work, the ability to save, and more free time. Also, many working-class people did not begin taking long holidays until the inter-war years, preferring to spend their leisure time at local attractions and on day trips, while customary holidays (for example bank holidays and towns' Wakes Weeks – when in the summer all industry would close) were used to provide hospitality to relatives and friends. Even by 1900 the vast majority of workers in the Potteries and the Black Country, for example, were still travelling only short distances for holidays, most going no further afield than Trentham Gardens or Sutton Park. Even after 1870, a trip to the seaside largely remained the preserve of the moneyed or a thrifty minority.

The fact that demand for seaside resorts amongst the working classes varied throughout Britain also highlights that the railway was not usually a decisive factor in their development. Proximity to a city or major town may have resulted in significant and ongoing development of resorts, which progressively catered for individuals wanting to take longer and longer seaside holidays. On the other hand, in the North-east, South Wales and the West of England – all areas that had good rail connections – resorts did not emerge to the same extent as elsewhere.

David Turner

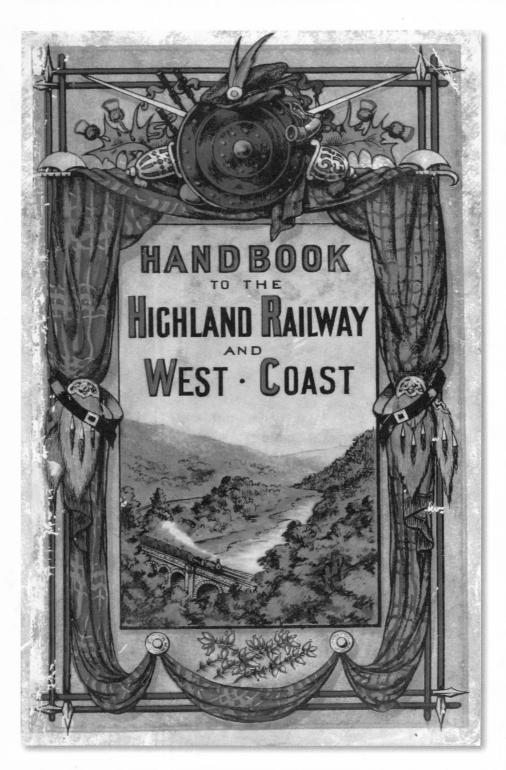

HANDBOOK
TO THE
HIGHLAND RAILWAY
AND
WEST · COAST

Monday
6

Tuesday
7

Wednesday
8

Thursday
9

Friday
10

Saturday
11

Sunday
12

Handbook to the Highland Railway for the 1890 summer season. (British Library Creative Commons)

INSTRUCTIONS TO RAILWAY TRAVELLERS

Proceed at once to the booking-office and procure a ticket for the class carriage you intend to travel by, and if near the time of starting, enter the departure shed.

Have your name legibly written on your luggage, and see it stowed away, and then take your seat in a carriage, carrying with you carpet bags or other light luggage, and wait till the starting bell rings.

Take care of your ticket to deliver at your journey's end, or to the attendant at starting, as the case may be.

The weight generally allowed to each passenger for luggage is about 100 lbs. and a charge is made for excess.

No smoking is allowed at the stations, nor in any of the carriages.

No dogs allowed to be taken inside the carriages, but they are conveyed in a proper vehicle at a small charge for each.

Do not leave your seat at any station, except the one at which refreshment is allowed, nor attempt to open the carriage doors yourself.

Females are in attendance at each terminus, and at the central refreshment station, to wait upon ladies and children.

Carriages and horses should be at the stations at least a quarter of an hour before the time of starting.

Post horses can always be obtained at each terminus and most of the stations.

Omnibuses, flys, coaches and cabs are always waiting the arrival of the trains at each terminus.

Children under ten years of age half-price, infants in arms, unable to walk, free of charge.

Every train is provided with guards and a conductor, who is responsible for the order and regularity of the journey.

Every guard, porter or policeman employed by the company has a distinguishing number on the collar of his coat.

The companies' servants are strictly enjoined, on pain of dismissal, to observe the utmost civility and attention towards all the passengers, nor are they to receive any fee or gratuity.

Henry Tuck, *Every Traveller's Guide to the Railways of England, Scotland, Ireland, Belgium, France, and Germany*, 1843

Monday

13

Tuesday

14

Wednesday

15

Thursday

16

Friday

17

Saturday

18

Father's Day

Sunday

19

GREAT WESTERN
RAILWAY

Royal Agricultural Society's Show
JUNE 23rd to 27th, 1903.
PARK ROYAL PERMANENT SHOW YARD,
LONDON.

On MONDAY, JUNE 22nd, 1903,

AN

EXCURSION TRAIN

FOR

LONDON

(PADDINGTON STATION)

WILL LEAVE		AT	Return Fares (Third Class).	Dates and Times of Return Trains.
		p.m.		
Clifton Down	... ...	5 14		Mondays, June 29th and July 6th, at 8.0 a.m.
Redland	... ...	5 16		
Montpelier	... ...	5 18	**12/-**	
Stapleton Road	... ...	5 45		Friday, July 3rd, at 7.35 p.m.
Lawrence Park	... ...	5 50		
St. Anne's Park	... ...	6 0		

Children under Three Years of Age, Free; Three and under Twelve, Half-price.
One Package of Luggage only allowed, which will be conveyed at Passenger's own risk.

The Tickets are not transferable. Should an Excursion or Cheap Ticket be used for any other Station than those named upon it, or by any other Train than those specified above, it will be rendered void, and therefore the fare paid will be liable to forfeiture, and the full Ordinary Fare will become chargeable.

PARK ROYAL SHOW GROUND WILL BE OPEN AS FOLLOWS :—

	a.m.	p.m.	Admission.		a.m.	p.m.	Admission
Tuesday, June 23rd ...	9.0 to	8.0	... 5/-	Thursday, June 25th ...	9.0 to	8.0	... 2/6
Wednesday, „ 24th ...	9.0 to	8.0	... 2/6	Friday, „ 26th ...	8.0 to	8.0	... 1/-

Saturday, June 27th ... 8.0 a.m. to 8.0 p.m. ... Admission 1/-
FOR MAP SEE OTHER SIDE.

For information respecting Tourist, Pleasure Party, and Excursion arrangements, and Special Trips on the Great Western Railway, application should be made to Mr. C. Kislingbury, Divisional Superintendent, Temple Meads Station, Bristol ; or at any of the Stations.

Paddington, June, 1903.　　　　　　　　**J. L. WILKINSON,** General Manager.

WYMAN & SONS, LTD., Printers, Fetter Lane, London, E.C., and Reading.—6593a.

Monday

20

Tuesday

21

Wednesday

22

Thursday

23

Friday

24

Saturday

25

Sunday

26

REFUSING CERTAIN PASSENGERS

A BYLAW

Except by special permission of the Company, a person suffering from any infectious or contagious disease or disorder shall not enter or remain or be in or upon the Company's premises, or in any carriage using the railway, or travel or attempt to travel on the railway; and the Company may refuse to receive or carry any such person, or to permit any such person to enter, remain or be in or upon any part of their premises, or in any such carriage, or to travel on the railway. Any person infringing or not observing this by-law and regulation may, without prejudice to the penalty prescribed by By-law No.1, be removed from the Company's premises, or from any such carriage, by or under direction of any servant or agent of the Company and shall be liable to the Company for the cost of disinfecting the Company's premises and any carriage in which such person shall have been, and to make good any other damage to the property of the Company through the infraction or non-observance of this by-law as well as to pay such penalty. Any person who has charge of any person so offending, or who aids or assists any such person in so offending, shall be deemed to infringe and offend against this by-law.

London & South Western Railway
Bylaws and Regulations, March 1905

Monday

27

Tuesday

28

Wednesday

29

Thursday

30

Friday

1

Saturday

2

Sunday

3

A REMARKABLE CLAIM

At a Sheriff's Court at Preston on Wednesday, damages were assessed in an extraordinary action for personal injuries. The plaintiff, a young lad named Day, residing at Oldham, was on the platform at Prestatyn Station, North Wales, on June 7, when the Irish Mail passed through at a rate of seventy miles an hour. Defendant, Walter Oldfield, a Liverpool clerk, who was in the train, threw out a bag of oranges, weighing 10 lbs, for his wife, who was also on the platform – the bag struck the plaintiff with a force estimated by experts as equal to 7 cwt. She was rendered unconscious and suffered shock to the system. The jury awarded £35 damages.

Cheltenham Chronicle, Saturday 19 August 1899

Prestatyn station, c. 1910.

Monday

4

Tuesday

5

Wednesday

6

Thursday

7

Friday

8

Saturday

9

Sunday

10

CARLISLE
Scotby
Camwhinton
Cotehill
Armathwaite
Lazonby
Longwathby
Alston
Allendale
Allenheads
Burnhill
Durham

New Biggin
Long Marton
Middleton
Bishop Auckland
Penrith
APPLEBY
Ormside
Barnard Castle
Stockton
Crosby Garrett
Darlington
Forcet
KIRKBY STEPHEN
Tebay
Richmond
Reeth
Leyburn
North...
Windermere
Low Gill
Kendal
Oxenholm
Hawes
Hawes Junc
Dent
Ribblehead
Masham
Haverthwaite
Lake side
Greenodd
Cark
Meals Bank
Grange
Arnside
Silverdale
Carnforth
Borwick
Arkholme
Wennington
Ingleton
Horton
Melmerby
Ulverston
Lindal
Dalton
Furness Abbey
Roose
Wennington
Clapham
SETTLE
Settle Junction
Pateley Bridge
Piel
Pier
MORECAMBE
Green Ayre
LANCASTER
Hornby
Caton
Halton
High Bentham
Giggleswick
Long Preston
Hellifield
Bell Busk
Gargrave
Skipton Junc
SKIPTON
Harrogate
ILKLEY
Ben Rhydding
Burley
Otley
Longridge
Thornton
Elslack
Gisburn
Barnoldswick
Barnoldswick Junc
Earby
Canonley
Kildwick
Steeton
Keighley
Menston
Baldon
Guiseley
Esholt
Calverley Br.
Kirkstall Forge
Kirkstall
Armley
LEEDS (Welling
Rothwell Hai
Chalburn
Foulridge
Ingrow
Damems
Oakworth
Haworth
Oxenhope
Bingley
Saltaire
Frizinghall
Manningham
Shipley
Holbeck
Hunslet
Woodleston
Methley
Preston
Colne
BRADFORD
Halifax
Dewsbury
Whitwood
Ardsley
Norm
Lytham
Burnley
Accrington
Todmorden
WAKEFIELD
Oakensh
Sandal
Southport
Blackburn
Bacup
Huddersfield
Rochdale
Royst
Cud
Ormskirk
Chorley
Burscough
Bolton
Bury
Monk Bretton
BARNSLEY
Darfield
Wigan
Rainford
Oldham
Darfield
Kilnhurst
MASBRO
Edge Hill
Holm
Hough Green
Farnworth
Sankey
WARRINGTON
Irlam
Flixton
Urmston
MANCHESTER
Ashton Staley Bridge
Guide Bridge
Hyde Junc.
Reddish
Belle Vue
Woodley
Romiley
MARPLE
Brightside
Attercliffe Road
SHEFFIELD
Ecclesall
Dore & Totley
LIVERPOOL
S. Michael
Otterspool
Mersey
GLAZEBROOK
Gadishead
Partington
West Timperley
Baguley
Northenden
Cheadle
STOCKPORT
Tiviotdale
Portwood
Bredbury
Hyde
New Mills
Bugsworth
Strines
Birch Vale
Hayfield
Chinley
Chapel le Frith
Woodhead
Penistone
Wath
Holme

Monday

11

Tuesday

12

Wednesday

13

Thursday

14

Friday

15

Saturday

16

Sunday

17

THE
EASTERN COUNTIES
RAILWAY COMPANY

OFFERS THE FOLLOWING ADVANTAGES TO
NERVOUS PERSONS.

Trains at REDUCED SPEED to meet their views.

The Rate of Speed is not at all FRIGHTFUL.

For example,—**Hertford** is 21 miles from LONDON by the road,—the time allowed for the second **business** train is **One Hour and Thirty-five Minutes!** *(but the journey is not always accomplished in that time.)* Again,—**Waltham** to LONDON was formerly done in **Thirty-seven Minutes**, the time now allowed is **Fifty-Eight Minutes.**

One of the Officials stated that **"The time allowed was so great that they did not know how to kill it!"**

MR. PUNCH says, " The only **Fast** trains on this Line are those that are **Stuck Fast."** These afford plenty of time for quiet reflection.

N.B.—A person offers for a Wager to run his Donkey against the Train for one stage, and have time for his Breakfast in the bargain!!!

The Season Tickets may be 10 or 20 per cent. higher than on other Lines, but as the time allowed for seeing the country is so liberal on the part of the Company, the Passengers must not complain. Railway Companies cannot afford to waste **Time** and **Steam** without being paid for it.

(By Authority)
PASSENGERS.

Monday

18

Tuesday

19

Wednesday

20

Thursday

21

Friday

22

Saturday

23

Sunday

24

This satirical flyer was published in 1852, mocking the quality of the Eastern Counties Railway's train services.
(Ian Dinmore)

THE RAILWAY
TERMINUS

There is certainly no more lively, bustling, animated and animating scene than the terminus of a railway on the departure of an express train. It does one good even to be an on-looker; and I can imagine that a man who has few opportunities to travel, might give himself a pleasant excitement every day, by visiting the nearest terminus to witness the excitement of others. In this ingenious manner I have enjoyed some delights of travelling, without the weariness of a journey, and without paying a fare. It would be difficult to describe what it is that renders the scene so invigorating. There seems to be a sort of animal magnetism at work. Everyone is excited though there is no particular cause for excitement. There are plenty of carriages, there are full five minutes to spare, and yet every individual on the platform is in an intense hurry – passing and repassing, darting at the book-stall, plunging into the refreshment-room, peeping into the carriages, glancing at the clock, asking questions of the guards (who are passing up and down with their hands slyly formed into money boxes), giving directions to porters, shaking hands with friends over and over again, and, if addicted to tobacco, making the most desperate efforts to avoid the ladies.

'Railway Thoughts', *All the Year Round*, 4 January 1868

Monday
25

Tuesday
26

Wednesday
27

Thursday
28

Friday
29

Saturday
30

Sunday
31

Summer bank holiday (Scotland)

Monday

I

Tuesday

2

Wednesday

3

Thursday

4

Friday

5

Saturday

6

Sunday

7

Willesden Junction High Level station before the First World War. (Tony Hisgett)

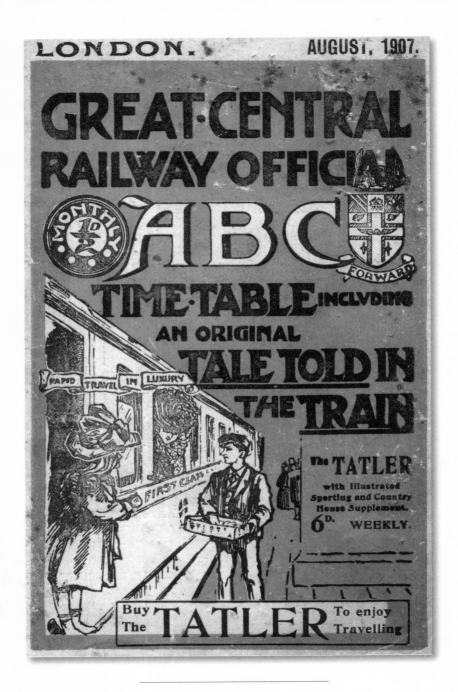

ABC Guides were different from *Bradshaw's Guides*. While *Bradshaw's* attempted to provide timetables for all Britain's trains, the *ABCs* listed the times only of trains running to and from London. They also carried fare information, which the *Bradshaw's* did not.

Monday
8

Tuesday
9

Wednesday
10

Thursday
11

Friday
12

Saturday
13

Sunday
14

SWINDON

SWINDON, on the Great Western, like Wolverton and Crewe on the North Western, is one of the extraordinary products of the railway enterprise of the present age. It is a colony of engineers and handicraft men. The company manufacture their own engines at the factory, where cleaning and everything connected with constructive repair is carried on.

The refreshment room at this station is admirably conducted, and abundantly supplied with every article of fare to tempt the best as well as the most delicate appetites, and the prices are moderate, considering the extortions to which travellers are occasionally exposed.

The valley of Stroud through which the railway passes from Swindon to Gloucester, is well known to travellers and tourists as presenting a continuous series of lovely landscapes. The valley is almost in the character of a mountain gorge, with a branching stream in the bottom, which partially furnishes the motive power for the numerous cloth and fulling mills of the district, the quality of the water, too, being peculiarly adapted for dyeing purposes.

Bradshaw's Handbook, 1863.

Monday

15

Tuesday

16

Wednesday

17

Thursday

18

Friday

19

Saturday

20

Sunday

21

The Engine House at Swindon, a lithograph by J. C. Bourne, 1846. (Science and Society Picture Library)

Above · Crewe station, *c.* 1900. (Tony Hisgett)

Inset · The *Bradshaw's Guide* was not the only source for timetables available to nineteenth-century railway travellers. *ABC Guides* listed the times of all trains to and from London, while the railway companies issued their own timetables.

Monday

22

Tuesday

23

Wednesday

24

Thursday

25

Friday

26

Saturday

27

Sunday

28

RAILWAY COMPANIONS

BY A DISAGREEABLE TRAVELLER

I HAVE come to the conclusion that the railway train exercises a sinister influence upon the human race. Persons who are tolerable or even welcome in ordinary daily life, become peculiarly obnoxious so soon as they enter the compartment of a train. No fairy prince ever stepped into a railway train, assuming he favoured that means of locomotion, without being transformed straightway into a Beast, and even Beauty herself could not be distinguished from her disagreeable sisters in a train.

Speaking for myself, railway travelling invariably brings to the surface all my worst qualities.

My neighbour opposite hazards some remark. I feel immediately a fit of taciturnity coming over me, and an overpowering inclination to retreat behind a fortification of journals and magazines. On the other hand, say that I have exhausted my stock of railway literature or, no remote possibility, that the literature has exhausted me then I make a casual remark about the weather. The weather is not usually considered a controversial topic: in railway trains, however, it becomes so.

'Rain! not a bit,' says a passenger in the far corner, evidently meditating a walking tour, and he views me suspiciously as if I were a rain-producer.

'And a good thing too,' remarks the man opposite. 'It's wanted badly, I tell you, sir, very badly. It's all very well for you holiday folk,' &c., &c.

And all this bad feeling because of my harmless well-intentioned remark.

The window is up. 'Phew! . . . stuffy,' says the man opposite. 'You don't mind, I hope, the window eh?' 'Not in the least,' I say, and conceive a deadly hatred for him. I know from experience that directly that window is down all the winds of heaven will conspire to rush through, bearing upon them a smoky pall. I resign myself, therefore, to possible bronchitis and inflammation of the eye... The window is down. 'W-h-oop,' coughs an elderly man. 'Do you mind, sir, that window being closed?' Polite mendacity and inward bitterness on my part towards the individual who has converted the compartment into an oven. But there are worse companions even than these, of whom I must speak another time.

From *Mr Punch's Railway Book*, 1905

Summer bank holiday (UK, exc Scotland)

Monday

29

Tuesday

30

Wednesday

31

Thursday

1

Friday

2

Saturday

3

Sunday

4

BRISTOL

The terminus of the railway is situated on an eminence rising from Temple Meads, where the two lines diverge respectively to London and Plymouth.

BRISTOL is a cathedral city, sea-port, and parliamentary borough in Gloucestershire, 118 miles from London, on the Great Western Railway... Its port is artificially made by excavating floating docks, 3 miles long, out of the old bed of the Avon (for which a new course was made), about 8 miles from King's Road in the Bristol Channel, the tide rising 40 to 50 feet. Since the tolls were reduced in 1848, the registered tonnage has risen to 71,000, and the foreign trade doubled. Much West India and Irish produce finds way into the country through this port. The chief manufactures are engines, glass, hats, pottery, soap, brushes, &c., besides various smaller branches, and a trade in sugar, rum, &c. This place has, from the earliest times, been an important seaport, from whence old navigators used to start. One of the foremost was Sebastian Cabot, a native, who sailed hence in 1497 to discover Labrador. Kidnapping, also, for the American plantations used to be practised here, and it shared with Liverpool in the iniquities of the slave trade. In the present day it is noted for having sent the first steamer across the Atlantic, the *Great Western* (Capt. Hosken), which sailed on the 2nd May, 1838, and reached New York in 15 days ... Coal and oolite are quarried.

Bradshaw's Handbook, 1863.

SEPTEMBER

Monday
5

Tuesday
6

Wednesday
7

Thursday
8

Friday
9

Saturday
10

Sunday
11

SCHOOLBOYS AND RAILWAY TRAVEL

The love of railway travelling is pretty universal with schoolboys. It has its mournful side when holidays come to an end, but I have a shrewd suspicion that a boy who has some 200 miles to journey back to school feels his spirits rise as the wonderful machine, of which he seems to form almost a part, rushes through county after county, carrying him to his fate. Of course, the holidays are the thing, but who can describe the boys going home for their holidays? ...I remember in my school days waiting at Derby, and losing many hours on the homeward journey to the South, to have the pleasure of travelling by a train then considered one of the best expresses in the day between Derby and Bristol. At the time of which I am speaking, the Midland had just introduced Pullman cars, and ran whole trains of them. Our delight, in those days was to stand on the balcony at the end of the cars. The rush through the air and the considerable risk to run increased the pleasure. Pullman cars, except a few sleepers, are less common now in England. I found myself in a Pullman dining car some seven years ago, and after dinner sought the balcony, as in days of old. It was very dark, but very enjoyable, and we took the points at some of the junctions like a racehorse. To me in this pleasant reverie enter the conductor. 'Very sorry, sir, but the company has given instructions to prevent passengers travelling outside of carriages, and the company will not be responsible in the case of accident.' This seemed reasonable enough, so I withdrew, but rather sadly. Travelling by night, that grand object of ambition to a boy who loves trains, has its romantic side, up to the age of twenty-two, especially in summer.

H. Stanley Tayler, *Railway Magazine,* January 1901

Monday

12

Tuesday

13

Wednesday

14

Thursday

15

Friday

16

Saturday

17

Sunday

18

THE OVERCROWDED CARRIAGE

·

Sir - An unfortunate omnibus conductor, if he admits on more passengers than his omnibus is licensed to carry, is invariably summoned and fined. Ought not the same law to be extended to the Metropolitan Railway Company? I travelled last night, between 11 and 11.20, from Victoria station to Praed-Street [Paddington], with a first-class ticket. There was a rush of passengers into the carriages. Some third-class, second-class, and few first-class, got into the same compartment where I was, only too glad to get standing room. The same thing occurred at every station we arrived at until Notting-hill, where there was a cessation of overcrowding. Between Sloane-street and the High-street Kensington, a well-dressed young lady (accompanied by a friend, fortunately for her) had to stand up while some of the not very clean third-class passengers, one evidently not sober, were occupying seats, into which were crammed six passengers on one side, and seven on the other. I expostulated with the guard of the train when I got out at Praed-street. His answer was 'I cannot help it, Sir.' Perhaps the directors of the Metropolitan Railway can help it either by putting on more carriages on their late trains, or causing their servants to more often examine the tickets of occupants of seats in first-class carriages. This is not the first or second time I have travelled in overcrowded first-class Metropolitan carriages; and a gentleman travelling in the same compartment with me informed me that overcrowding was a constant occurrence by late trains and especially on Sunday nights.

I am, your obedient servant.

A FIRST CLASS PASSENGER

The Times, Tuesday, 31 October 1871

Monday

19

Tuesday

20

Wednesday

21

Thursday

22

Friday

23

Saturday

24

Sunday

25

The Midland Railway was the first company to introduce luxurious Pullman carriages into Britain from America in 1876. This is the interior of one of those carriages in 1883. On their arrival into the service the *Sheffield Independent* described their interiors as being 'luxuriant ... the roof ... is raised in the centre, and illuminated with some of the most artistic distemper painting, while the airy and light build gives it a handsome general appearance.' (Picture: The Internet Archive)

Monday

26

Tuesday

27

Wednesday

28

Thursday

29

Friday

30

Saturday

1

Sunday

2

NOT MUCH NEED FOR 'LADIES ONLY' COMPARTMENTS

·

Some 20 railway companies in the United Kingdom have replied to the Board of Trade circular calling attention to the advisability of providing separate compartments for female passengers. The Cheshire Lines Committee state that their instructions to reserve a compartment in each class of carriage by each train for ladies desirous of travelling alone had been invariably carried out, and there could be no cause of complaint. As a rule, however, ladies did not avail themselves of these compartments. Whilst they had every intention of continuing this arrangement for long journeys, it was a question whether there was any real necessity for it on short-distance trains... The London North-Western Company say it has been their custom for many years to reserve compartments in all their main line trains in third-class carriages and to a limited extent also in first and second class carriages ... there was a disinclination on the part of ladies to use these compartments because they were used by nurses travelling with children, as well as children travelling alone. The Lancashire and Yorkshire Railway Company say they made the arrangement some years ago, but it was very little used. They set apart compartments for ladies on all the trains between Liverpool, Crosby, and Southport. The Manchester, Sheffield, and Lincolnshire Company state that they do not as a rule reserve compartments, but that station-masters and guards have instructions to afford the accommodation when asked for. The Great Western Railway Company reply to the same effect and add that the special accommodation provided is largely in excess of requirements. The Midland Company say that compartments are reserved for ladies when specially asked for, and this is found to be sufficient.

Manchester Courier and Lancashire General Advertiser, Saturday, 25 February 1888

Monday

3

Tuesday

4

Wednesday

5

Thursday

6

Friday

7

Saturday

8

Sunday

9

TRAVELLING FOR SPORT

_⌒ • ⌒_

It is very easy to assume that the growth in popularity of sporting events in the nineteenth century was the result of railways enabling spectators to travel over great distances to support their favourite team or sportsperson. Particular examples supporting this idea are easy to find. The railways brought sixty thousand people to Crystal Palace in 1907 for the FA Cup Final, while they increased the spectatorship at prize fights by putting on special trains.

In reality the trend of increasing attendance at sporting events had begun before 1830, before the advent of the railways. Horse-racing is a prime example. In the 1810s York races could attract 100,000 and Manchester races pulled in 150,000. Crowds at Epsom in the 1820s and 1830s regularly reached 200,000. Yet, similar numbers attended race meetings after the railway arrived. They simply took over the role that other modes of travel, such as stagecoaches and walking, had carried out previously. Only in exceptional cases did the railways increase the numbers of people attending racecourses, for example where a race was of national interest. For a race at Doncaster in 1887 special trains came from as far away as London, Birmingham, Liverpool, Barrow, Carlisle, Newcastle, Chester, Bristol and King's Lynn.

The long distances these spectators travelled on these special trains were the exception not the rule: most of those attending sporting events came from the local area. For instance, most of those going to rowing meetings in the North-east in the 1880s came from that region. The short distances spectators usually travelled also meant that most did not use the railway for their journeys to sporting venues. In 1901 only sixty to seventy thousand people travelled to the Epsom races by train; a larger number came by motor car, bus or on foot, and thus could be considered to have lived close to the course.

From the 1870s crowds at the increasingly popular team sports – football and rugby – were also mostly from the teams' surrounding area. Football supporters usually walked to games and from the 1890s the tram, and not the train, became their preferred method of travel. There were, however, exceptions. By 1912 the Great Eastern Railway was conveying forty thousand home fans to Tottenham Hotspur games from parts of north London. Generally, however, away fans were not a feature of matches before 1914, except when there was a derby. The majority of football fans were working-class and were unable to afford the train tickets to attend away matches regularly, and in an era when most employed individuals worked on Saturday mornings they lacked the time to travel the hundreds of miles

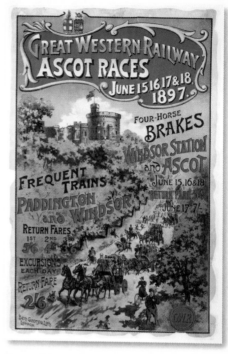

(Science and Society Picture Library)

to get to them. Mass movement of away fans usually occurred only when the stakes of a particular game were high, for example regional and national cup finals and semi-finals.

On the other hand, the railways were vital in increasing the participation in sport over the Victorian period by widening opportunities for people, particularly from the upper and middle classes, to become involved. Moreover, the provision of cheap transport led to the professionalisation of some sports and widened the opportunities for sportsmen to compete in prestige competitions.

Before the railway age sportsmen travelled throughout Britain in search of competitions and 'national champions' were created. In the 1830s a champion jockey, Tommy Lye, travelled 6,000 miles by horse and coach to ride in 173 races. A spreading railway network enabled his successors to compete in considerably more races. In the 1840s and 1850s jockeys took part in between 250 and 350 races yearly; while by the early 1900s top riders were taking part in six to eight hundred races. Pugilists, pedestrians,

A Glasgow & South Western Railway bookmark from about 1911 promoting travel to the golf resorts along its line. (Science and Society Picture Library)

rowers and even wrestlers also travelled more from the 1840s as a direct result of railway development. Those wishing to participate in more solitary sports – wildfowling and fishing – could also access the countryside more easily and cheaply because of the railway, while pigeon-racing emerged because pigeons could be sent greater distances quickly. By the 1890s golf clubs at seaside resorts such as Lytham St Anne's, Hoylake and Southport realised the value of golf traffic for visitor numbers and put on golf competitions to attract residents and weekend golfers, most of whom arrived by train.

For whole teams the cost and time involved in travelling to faraway games by means other than the railway, such as stagecoaches, would have been prohibitive if they played many matches over a season. The railways therefore had their biggest impact on the growth of participation in team sports, again by reducing the cost and increasing the speed of transport. The first team sport to benefit from the railways was cricket. From the 1840s onwards teams began touring, and William Clarke's All England eleven, and then two other professional sides, went all over the country playing matches.

'Going North, King's Cross Station', from 1893, shows passengers gathered at the station, with their dogs, guns and sporting equipment, ready to catch a train to Scotland at the beginning of the game-shooting season in August.

The railways played their biggest role in the development of football and rugby from the 1870s onwards. Firstly, they facilitated communication and connections between practitioners of these developing sports. Teams could travel far to play games, and short journeys became quicker, enabling more out-of-town fixtures to be played. The more famous teams

Going North, King's Cross Station, *from 1893, shows passengers gathered at the station, with their dogs, guns and sporting equipment, ready to catch a train to Scotland at the beginning of the game-shooting season in August. (Science and Society Picture Library)*

by the 1880s were even conducting Easter and Christmas tours. Refinement and formalisation of rules and techniques naturally followed from the sharing of ideas. Alongside this, the railways facilitated the growth of formal football associations and leagues. Initially the Football League recruited teams to it on the basis of their distance from a station: Sunderland did not join for many years because the Midland clubs felt that transportation costs to the town were excessive.

Despite the improved transport connections the railways provided, not every team's train got them to matches on time. Many clubs had to shorten, postpone and cancel games before 1900 because of failures by the railway network. In 1874 – a period when the rules of football were still evolving – a football match between Durham School and Stockton was shortened from four twenty-minute quarters to fifty minutes owing to the 'usual unpunctuality of the North Eastern Railway, the train reaching Durham fully half an hour late'.

Overall, the effect of the coming of the railways on sport in Britain was mixed. On the one hand, it did not have a dramatic effect on spectatorship – changes in this direction being the result of other factors. On the other, the railways widened and encouraged participation by the populace in a whole range of sports and contributed to the professionalisation of others.

David Turner

ESCAPE OF A PRISONER FROM A TRAIN

•

A man named Daniel Docherty was remitted to the Sheriff from yesterday's Port-Glasgow Police Court on a charge of stealing a watch and chain. He was in the course of the day being removed to Greenock with another prisoner, when he suddenly sprang through the railway carriage window and effected his escape. The train was only a short distance from Port Glasgow station at the time, and was proceeding at a slow rate. Docherty, who is an old offender, was handcuffed to his fellow-prisoner, and by some means managed to withdraw his hand from the iron.

Edinburgh Evening News, Thursday 14 June 1883

(Tony Harden)

Monday
10

Tuesday
11

Wednesday
12

Thursday
13

Friday
14

Saturday
15

Sunday
16

COMPLAINTS AGAINST THE SOUTH WESTERN

·

The most humorous piece of writing in the world is to be seen on the South-Western Railway between Fulwell and Twickenham. It is on a board, and the quaint, incisive words are, 'Speed not to exceed ten miles an hour.' Even people with urgent appointments, the keeping of which means life and death as they dodder up to town at the old Thames Valley speed of four and a half miles an hour, have to shriek with laughter when they read Archibald Scott's great joke. People tell with bated breath how there was once an engine-driver, appropriately termed Dare Devil Dick, who got six miles an hour out of a Thames Valley train, and was seen by a director, and was sacked for furious driving, and was hired by the Midland and sacked for slowness, and now, having qualified on the S.W.R., is earning an honest livelihood by driving a hearse.

The Sporting Times, Saturday, 29 October 1881

I travel and have travelled over almost all the lines in Europe ... there is not one so badly managed as the South-Western, nor is there any time table which is so purely the work of supposition.

Lindo S. Myers

Within the past three years I have made upwards of 180 long-distance journeys on this line to Devon, Dorset and Hants, and in one case only have we ever kept time. Usually the trains are later than the hours given in the time tables by 15 to 20 minutes, and in very many cases considerably more, with the result that other trains are perpetually missed and engagements constantly broken.

H. Stopes

The Times, Tuesday, 21 October 1884

Monday

17

Tuesday

18

Wednesday

19

Thursday

20

Friday

21

Saturday

22

Sunday

23

Railway construction through nineteenth-century cities demolished huge numbers of houses, the large majority of which were of poor quality or were slums. The result was the forced removal of thousands of the poorest in society from their homes. An estimate is that fifty-one railway schemes between 1853 and 1885 displaced 56,000 people in London, with 37,000 of these evictions occurring in the eight years between 1859 and 1867. It was not until late in the century that the railway companies were legally obliged to re-house those they had uprooted, and so all were forced to find their own accommodation. Intially the opinion was that they would move into the outer areas of cities, yet the reality was that the newly homeless usually moved into even smaller local accommodation, so as to remain close to work, further worsening their living conditions. (British Library Creative Commons)

Monday

24

Tuesday

25

Wednesday

26

Thursday

27

Friday

28

Saturday

29

Sunday

30

DICKENS AND THE OLDER TRAVELLER

In the same carriage with me there sat an ancient gentleman (I feel no delicacy in alluding to him, for I know that he is not in the room, having got out far short of Birmingham), who expressed himself most mournfully as to the ruinous effects and rapid spread of railways, and was most pathetic upon the virtues of the slow-going old stage coaches. Now I, entertaining some little lingering kindness for the road, made shift to express my concurrence with the old gentleman's opinion, without any great compromise of principle. Well, we got on tolerably comfortably together, and when the engine, with a frightful screech, dived into some dark abyss, like some strange aquatic monster, the old gentleman said it would never do, and I agreed with him. When it parted from each successive station, with a shock and a shriek as if it had had a double-tooth drawn, the old gentleman shook his head, and I shook mine. When he burst forth against such new-fangled notions, and said no good could come of them, I did not contest the point. But I found that when the speed of the engine was abated, or there was a prolonged stay at any station, up the old gentleman was at arms, and his watch was instantly out of his pocket, denouncing the slowness of our progress.

Charles Dickens, speech at Conversazione of the Polytechnic Institution, Birmingham, 28 February 1844

OCTOBER – NOVEMBER

Halloween

Monday

31

Tuesday

1

Wednesday

2

Thursday

3

Friday

4

Saturday

5

Sunday

6

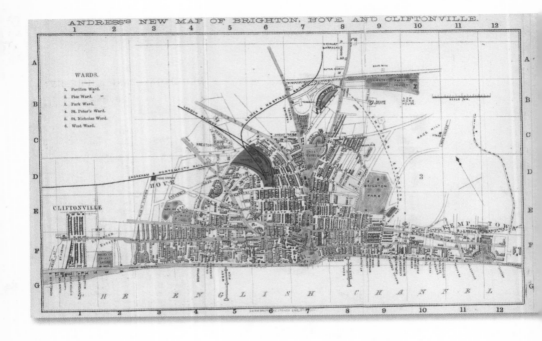

BRIGHTON

The BRIGHTON TERMINUS is an elegant structure, fitted up in the most convenient manner. There is a portico in the Roman architectural style, which projects on pillars into the street, and is surmounted by an illuminated clock.

This once famous resort of royalty and fashion may now, through the literal as well as metaphorical levelling of the railroad, be fairly entitled to the appellation of the Marine Metropolis. Merchants who formerly made Dulwich or Dalston the boundaries of their suburban residences, now have got their mansions on the south coast, and still get in less time, by a less expensive conveyance, to their counting-houses in the city. Excursions are now made with greater facility, and possibly more enjoyment, to Brighton, than would have, a few years back, sufficed for the common-place pilgrimage to Hampton Court; and a constant succession of trains, conveying a host of pleasure-seekers and business men to and fro, now traverse with marvellous frequency and precision the line that has sprung, by the magical enterprise of man, from tracts of waving corn-fields and boundless breadths of pasture.

Bradshaw's Handbook, 1863.

Monday

7

Tuesday

8

Wednesday

9

Thursday

10

Friday

11

Saturday

12

Sunday

13

HIDING IN A RAILWAY CARRIAGE

A RISKY METHOD OF CHEAP TRAVELLING

At Carlisle Police Court, three sporting men, giving the names of Henry, Maxwell and Cousin, were charged with travelling on the London and North-Western Railway from Preston to Carlisle without having paid their fares. The evidence showed that the men, who belong to Manchester, took tickets from Manchester to Preston by one of the night expresses in order to go to Carlisle for the Border Union Coursing Meeting at Longtown. When the train got to Carlisle a ticket-examiner looked in a third class lavatory compartment, but, seeing no one, passed on to collect tickets in the next compartment. Hearing a slight noise, however, he returned to the compartment and found seven men in it. They had concealed themselves in the lavatory, and were waiting for a chance to leave the train unobserved. When questioned they said the guard had their tickets; but as this was false, the officials turned them out. All seven men bolted, and only the three named above were captured. Inquiry showed that they had given wrong names and addresses, one address being a whitewashed cottage, where an old lady lived who knew nothing about the prisoner. Another gave the address of his mother where he had not lived for years. It was alleged that Henry's real name was David Davidson, and that he was a well-known railway thief. Each prisoner was fined 40s, and costs. Another man named Augustus Parton, for attempting to travel with a ticket twelve months old from Carlisle to Manchester, was also fined 40s, and costs.

Dundee Courier, Tuesday 3 November 1896

Monday

14

Tuesday

15

Wednesday

16

Thursday

17

Friday

18

Saturday

19

Sunday

20

Two 'races to the north' had taken place between the companies operating the East and West Coast routes to Scotland in 1888 and 1895. In the event of further races, the North Eastern Railway (NER) wished to be prepared and built two locomotives, classified Q1, in 1896. Because of the need for speed, the locomotives had the largest coupled driving wheels of any British locomotive; they were 7 feet 7.25 inches in diameter. No further 'races' occurred, but the locomotives did put in some impressive runs during their lives. On a rainy day around 1900, no. 1869 ran the 44.25 miles from Darlington to York in 42 minutes 7 seconds with a load of 200 tons. This was an average speed of 61.7 mph, with a maximum speed of 74 mph at Tollerton. This is its sister locomotive, no. 1870, resting outside York around 1905.

Monday

21

Tuesday

22

Wednesday

23

Thursday

24

Friday

25

Saturday

26

Sunday

27

THE LOST PROPERTY DEPARTMENT

•

... an enormous amount of trouble is taken by the Lost Property Department of a railway company to collect the various articles at a given point where travellers can conveniently call, identify and re-claim their property; yet many things which undoubtedly were of value to their owners remain unclaimed and fall under the hammer of the auctioneer at the periodical sales. The reason why some hundreds of thousands of people, for instance, should fail to claim umbrellas, which readily sell under the hammer in bundles of a dozen each at 24s per bundle, is hard to explain. It is quite easy to understand that people leave umbrellas in trains by accident; but why having lost them, do they fail to apply and secure their return? One could almost fill a book of questions provided by a railway lost-property sale. What, for instance, induced a mysterious man to appear at a country station and deposit on the platform two large blocks of cherry-wood, each of considerable value, but without any address or particulars attached. And supposing that he left the station under the impression that he had duly ticketed them with the address to which they were to be sent, why were no inquiries eventually made? Perhaps the loss of gloves is more easily understood, for they are not of sufficient value to induce most people to bother about applying to the Lost Property Department. Hence the patient officials are called upon to collect some ten thousand pairs, to stuff them in giant sacks, and offer them to all and sundry for what they may fetch. But the explanation of comparative worthiness cannot be extended to articles of jewellery, which form a prominent part in every sale, considering that upon auction some of these items fetch as much as six or seven pounds, and one is forced back upon the same inquiry - why did the owners not apply?

Pall Mall Magazine, August 1909

Monday

28

Tuesday

29

St Andrew's Day (Scotland) Wednesday

30

Thursday

1

Friday

2

Saturday

3

Sunday

4

In this picture of Stoke-on-Trent station around 1900, we see many of the features that made up the hustle and bustle of stations in this period. The porter on the right minds a wagon load of baskets, perhaps waiting for a passenger or trader to collect them. We will never know what they contained, but it could be anything from petticoats to pigeons to potatoes. In the centre of the picture passengers weave their way around milk-churns. Whether empty or full, these illustrate that milk was usually delivered daily to town and city stations to supply the populace. A girl stands with a summer hat on; possibly she was waiting for a train that will whisk her to the seaside. By the late nineteenth century the local 'resort' for Stoke was Blackpool, whither thousands of holidaymakers and excursionists flocked yearly. Finally, the man on the left, seeing his train in, holds in his hand a newspaper or periodical. After 1870, the growth in the readership of periodicals, sold at most stations, in many cases by W.H. Smith, was aided by an explosion in passenger numbers at the same time. Simply put, people needed something easy to read on the train.

Monday

5

Tuesday

6

Wednesday

7

Thursday

8

Friday

9

Saturday

10

Sunday

11

THE CHRISTMAS TRAIN

It was no use to try and sweep the snow away from the pavement in front of the terminus of the London, Somesham, and Allover Railway: so they gave it up. But in spite of the rate at which the snow fell and drifted into heaps, it was doubtful whether it came faster than the passengers; and at last, as if beaten in the conflict, the snow ceased to fall, and for a while the intending travellers had it all their own way. On foot, and in every description of vehicle, they came; and one trainful was only despatched to make room for another; while as the early evening shades began to fall, and the gas to glimmer here and there, the noise, bustle and confusion became greater than ever.

There was no mistake about it — they were busy in the great terminus; porters rushing hither and thither; barrows were being driven like reaping machines amongst the standing human corn; passengers, smothered in every description of wrapper, panted about like resuscitated mummies. Seats were found and lost again; luggage was placed in the wrong vans; first-class passengers were thrust in second-class carriages, and *vice versa*. Chaos seemed to reign in the land of order; and the platform inspector, after running about and shouting till he was hoarse, stood still, and blew his nose in despair.

The engine had been long in its place, hissing and snorting loudly, as if impatient to be off; and guard and driver had again and again referred to their great open-faced silver watches ... There was the last bang of the door, the piping of the whistle, a triumphant screech from the engine, followed by a loud puff, when there came a jerk ... as the train began to glide along the platform ... amidst a general chorus of 'We're off at last,' the second-class passenger leaned out for an instant to draw back his head powdered with snow.

Bow Bells Annual quoted in *Wrexham Advertiser*
— Saturday, 25 December 1869

Monday
12

Tuesday
13

Wednesday
14

Thursday
15

Friday
16

Saturday
17

Sunday
18

Monday

19

Tuesday

20

Wednesday

21

Thursday

22

Friday

23

Saturday

24

Christmas Day

Sunday

25

A NINETEEN HOUR WAIT FOR RESCUE

Sir - Will you allow me to exercise my constitutional privilege of grumbling through your columns? I am one of the many hundreds of passengers who were blocked up in a snow-drift near Oxford on Tuesday night. It is bad enough to have spent 19 hours in a railway cutting under such circumstances, and nine hours more in the overcrowded waiting-rooms of a roadside station; but is much worse, and to my mind reprehensible, that the railway authorities in London should have taken no means to relieve the anxieties of the passengers' friends as to their safety. On my return, I found that my wife had sent no less than five times yesterday to Paddington, and all the information she could get was that the train was blocked up in a snow-drift, but that they could not say whether the passengers had been got out or not, and it was not until 10 p.m. that she could ascertain that the passengers were safe. I understand that many more anxious inquirers were treated in the same way.

Insomuch as the train was emptied by 10 a.m., the block having occurred before 5 p.m. the previous evening, it is impossible that the railway authorities in London could have been ignorant of the real state of affairs, and a placard in the station would have spared much distress.

Will you allow me to take this opportunity of expressing my thanks, which I am sure my fellow passengers would gladly share in, to the Rev. Lord Alwyne Compton, to the vicar of Radley, to the Head Master of Radley College, and to several other gentlemen in the neighbourhood whose names I am unacquainted with, for their kind and prompt services in organizing relief parties, and supplying such food as they could procure to the passengers? By so doing, I do not doubt that they saved many delicate women and children from the really serious consequences that might have followed a night's exposure in such bitter cold, and had the railway authorities in Oxford emulated them in promptitude, much suffering may have been avoided.

I am, &c.

W.S.P.

The Times, Saturday, 22 January 1881